Walking With Time

Walking With Time
Nicholas Lyon Gresson

ARCADIA

Daddy was first published in *Poems for Our Time: A Brookfield Press Anthology*, Brookfield Press, Auckland, 1985; and republished in *A Life In Poetry: Nicholas Lyon Gresson*, edited by Elizabeth Grierson, Arcadia imprint, Australian Scholarly Publishing Pty Ltd, North Melbourne, 2011.

Peach and Cherub and *For the Child* were first published in *A Life In Poetry: Nicholas Lyon Gresson*, edited by Elizabeth Grierson, Arcadia imprint, Australian Scholarly Publishing Pty Ltd, North Melbourne, 2011.

© Nicholas Lyon Gresson 2013
First published 2013
Arcadia, the general books' imprint of
Australian Scholarly Publishing Pty Ltd
7 Lt Lothian St Nth, North Melbourne, Vic., 3500
TEL: 03 9329 6963 FAX: 03 9329 5452
EMAIL: aspic@ozemail.com.au WEB: scholarly.info

Design and typesetting: Sarah Anderson
Printing and binding: BPA Pty Ltd

Cover image: *Carlton Gardens Melbourne*. Photo: Nicholas Gresson 2013.

This collection of poems is dedicated to Elizabeth Mary Grierson
to honour her deep beauty and skilled insights. She has been a constant
companion sustaining every word I have written.
And I would like to acknowledge the debt of gratitude I owe to her
parents Hugh and Olive Botting.

Contents

Acknowledgements

To Vi and Richard Cottrell of Christchurch for their generosity over the years, and to Carole Ann and Tony Mountfort of Mt Maunganui. I remember Bob and Mary Watson of Wellington for the warm times we shared, and 'Granny' Queenie Jones of Mt Maunganui for cups of tea and kindness. And for much appreciated contact I acknowledge C. K. Stead, my neighbour in Tohunga Crescent, Parnell, Auckland.

Foreword

Elizabeth M. Grierson

Nicholas Lyon Gresson was born in Fendalton, Christchurch, New Zealand, on 19 December 1939. Here he lived his first 16 years to 1956 when his father was appointed Judge of the Supreme Court (now High Court) Auckland and the family moved to *Stoneways*, Mountain Road, Epsom. His schooling was at Medbury Preparatory School and Christ's College in Christchurch, with a final year at King's College Auckland in 1957.

With an unusual deviation from the profession of law that had characterised the Gresson family over several generations – his great-great grandfather Henry Barnes Gresson being the earliest Judge of Canterbury, his grandfather Maurice James Gresson turning down invitations to the Bench three times, and his father Terence Arbuthnot Gresson, at 42 years of age, becoming a very young appointment to the Supreme Court – Nicholas followed a lively practical bent in engineering and travelled the world: first to Australia where he confirmed his love of adventure working as a ship's engineer at Evans Deakin Shipyard in Brisbane, and buying an Olivetti 32 typewriter to take on a journey north as far as Cairns. There he discovered a little coastal trader *M.V. Poseidon* that was working from an inlet outside of Cairns and a Captain Shipway gave him a job loading and unloading cement bags; and in September 1963 on the *Poseidon* he found himself on Thursday Island in the Torres Strait, where the free spirit there had been waiting to encompass him. Unfortunately the twelve-day manuscript he wrote, *Voyage to Thursday Island* was later stolen on a trip to England aboard the *Ellinis*.

In those Australian days there were also adventures across the Nullabor Plain travelling twice by train as far as Perth where he celebrated his twenty-third birthday. Some of his paintings were exhibited there, at the Hovea Gallery. It was on the *M. V. Patris* bound for Piraeus that he began writing poetry in earnest, and illuminating short stories, such as *The Dive*, on a typewriter lent to him by the ship's purser. Throughout 1964 he lived in England where he worked as a personnel trainee at Hoover Ltd in Perivale near London. Then for two years, he used his practical skills as engineer on many German ships working numerous passages up and down the east coasts of North and South America.

With an affinity for the strange and new (which his father Terence protected eloquently in him) and meeting the poverty in cities like Santos and along the railway tracks from Buenos Aires, he saw and experienced life in a way that could later find form in writing. In 1966 and 1967, he made return visits from New Zealand to Thursday Island, as he had promised himself in 1963, working as a taxi driver on land and going out to sea with the pearling luggers on the mother-craft to bring back the pearl-shells gathered by the divers – his job to hang the shells in the sea-water holds.

After the death of his father in November 1967, and with travels behind him, marriage and family called. While living on the hill at Sumner, near Christchurch, he worked as wages clerk at the Lyttelton Waterfront Industry Commission; and there, in Christchurch, in February 1971 his daughter Justine was born. From 1972 to 1982 he lived with his wife and young family at Mt Maunganui, his son Emerson being born at Tauranga in January 1974. At this time he worked as wages clerk at the AFFCO Cool Store on the Mt Maunganui wharf and enjoyed fishing for kingfish in the Tauranga Harbour and trips out to Mayor Island, and many runs up and around the Mount to train for the annual King of the Mountain Race.

Following the death of his son Emerson in 1982, he returned to Christchurch where he bought a house near the running track of Canterbury University, Ilam, but his marriage had run its course. He has been living in Auckland for the past 25 years, still with a love of adventure through travelling and engaging the intersections of life's variations and human expectations. In 1999, while living in Brighton,

England, he was awarded a Queen's Service Medal for his work counselling and assisting those in psychological difficulties, and working alongside the police for community safety against drugs.

Nicholas has long engaged the art of photography, starting with the family cats and dogs at *Gartmore,* his family home in Christchurch, and he continues to mediate life and environment through the camera lens and publish in a range of art magazines, art catalogues and websites. He has also maintained his love of following sport and a life-long passion for motor racing, bringing together his aesthetic and mechanical sensibilities – and it is here he mirrors that Ayrton Senna focus on the unexpected forces and corners of a well-examined life.

His life is marked also by a love of law, an inescapable imprint from his family, and from earliest years an interest in the vicissitudes of the human mind through criminal cases. Law and psychology met serendipitously for him when his father was called upon to defend one of the girls in the Parker-Hulme murder trial in Christchurch – recorded well in the 2011 book by lawyer Peter Graham, *So Brilliantly Clever: Parker, Hulme and the murder that shocked the world,* which includes a September 1954 photograph Nicholas took when he was 14 years old, of Hilda Marion Hulme at the Christchurch Airport (Harewood) with her lover, Bill Perry, leaving the country for England "while her daughter languished in jail" (Graham, 2011).

With a passionate sense of justice and the need for evidence to be scrutinised and properly dealt with, he worked with lawyer friends on many legal cases in Auckland. This includes the famous Arthur Allan Thomas case, where his work for justice is clearly encapsulated in *All the Commissioner's Men: Inside the Crewe murders inquiry,* by Chris Birt, published in 2012. In the acknowledgements to that book, Birt wrote, "*To my old travelling companion Nick, who regardless of the passage of time, has continued to insist that justice must be done for those persons and those families who were robbed of that by a system he loved and cherished...*".

And through it all Nicholas, the writer, was honing the craft of poetry and recording through words his life and times. Since 2005 he has worked at his poetry both at home in Auckland, New Zealand, and in

Melbourne, Australia, where he has found inspiration in the parks and gardens, the crowded trams and cafés, and along the banks of the Yarra. In 2011, *A Life In Poetry: Nicholas Lyon Gresson* attracted warm interest and some profound responses.

This collection *Walking With Time* is his second book of poetry.

Nicholas Lyon Gresson QSM
Ohakune New Year
Photo: Elizabeth Grierson 2012

Spinning the Diamond

Elizabeth M. Grierson

This new book of poetry by Nicholas Lyon Gresson called *Walking With Time* could quite easily be called 'Honouring the Word'. Reading the poems aloud one can feel the momentum of words: they push around each other, settling for an often unexpected conclusion in the last line or two. His words light up the mundane, life's constant circle of ordinariness – his place in the scheme of things, a place that is as much ignoble as it is noble, an ordinary man living an ordinary life, gathering and observing as he goes.

Following *A Life In Poetry*, launched in Melbourne, September 2011, which covered 55 years of writing, *Walking With Time* brings together 18 months of writing in various locations in New Zealand and Australia, with the inclusion of a few from earlier times. In formulating this introduction I reflect on how the poems have been written, how they come into being. They are not born fully-formed; they take work, each word particular to the next and each line disclosing more, adding texture to the underlying theme. Perhaps this is what a 'poetic sensibility' is? But that term may sound grandiose. Poetry is a craft; it's a practice that becomes a way of encapsulating life; for the poet it is a meaning for life, devoid of other trappings, meeting the demands of the poetic ahead of other expectations.

How does the poem find a life in itself? The poet is not separated from the world, but observes from within it, allowing the world's significances to reverberate, scratching the surface of imagination to access partial memories and bring them to the present. Language is the power; the poet's ego does not intervene – in fact to create there is a kind of suspension of control, a bending of language and an acute watching of the structure and the considered placement of words, their juxtaposition, all in the service of a pulse to carry the movement of language, the emerging focus of thought, the evocation of emotion. This process I have watched; and through the whole process I have seen this poet hold to the idea of the poem as it becomes part of his daily life until dealt with through words. My observation is that he holds onto a sense of wonder as he crafts the growing poem. As New Zealand writer and literary critic, C. K. Stead said, "I think of writing a poem as putting oneself in the moment, at the moment – an action more comprehensive, intuitive and mysterious than mere thinking..." (The Poetry Archive).

. But I note there is a difficulty to see the 'poetic' as a value in today's market-driven world where everything is turned into a commodity, even thought and emotion. So much is concrete now. In Melbourne at the time of the launch of *A Life In Poetry*, a newspaper reporter asked me this question, "Is poetry still thriving as an artform? Is it still relevant?" and I answered, "I think it is. People have their own way into poetry. People look for the poetic in something." At the same time I think the concept of the poetic as a part of life can be misunderstood; it gets invalidated as there is no room for it – the aesthetic itself is being denied, the aesthetic is under attack, worn down under the weight of other priorities, so it gets squeezed out. Yet the poetic is continually around us; it is neither foppish nor stand-offish, neither sugar nor angst, it is *there* for us to find. Poetry is an interruption to the attachments, to the cacophony of noise in which we are immersed. The poet brings many elements together in a kaleidoscope of sound and meaning, letting the words take over.

I once asked Nick, "Is this form of writing hard work, a form of agony, or is it pleasurable hard work?" He said:

> I love it. It is all and both. Like motor racing words can run off
> the track easily, so you have to be alert, aware of the forces around
> you, listen to the words, see escape routes, surrender at times. It is
> astonishing how open it is, and from so many sides the words can
> come... *the emotion finds itself.* You just keep running with it all

and you have to keep up. There's no prescribed 'poetic', but when it works, it works poetically.

Nick believes in the sharing of the poetic voice and is very alive to other poets' writings. I am reminded of what Pulitzer Prize winner and US Poet Laureate 1995–97 Robert Hass said, "Poets are always taking and giving from each other, poetry is an enormous pot luck in that way." When Nick first discovered the poetry of Frederico Garcia Lorca in Buenos Aires 1965, he found an everyday sensibility in Lorca's writing, and a similar attraction to the Chilean poet Pablo Neruda. Here was a way to address the ordinary of life freed from the mire of morality and heroic sensibility. He found they stirred his own anti-intellectual approach to perceiving everyday reality where the small things like a cup of coffee or a flower on a path could hold their place and purpose. Perhaps this is exemplified in his poem *A Day in the Life of* where he writes, *I lever myself / gather up my glasses and newspaper... / remember my watch / and the time / the black and white dress.*

The final poem in *A Life In Poetry,* Nick's previous book, concerned the Christchurch earthquake of February 2011. The poem, and the book, ended with these evocative words: *And I shall be a stranger in my sleep / spreading down a quilt of prayers.* He didn't stop there. The first poem in this book starts: *So I stood listening / and before me a voice.* These words turn the reader from loss to anticipation. A heightened sense of noticing invites a willing intersection with what is before us and behind us; and from this starting point the mind can safely wander *alone* in time and place, even to those distant *soundless childhood hours.*

This collection, arranged in two parts, spins the diamond of life's small and large moments. The poems were largely written in 2011 and 2012, with the exception of *To Dylan Thomas* 1970, *Peach and Cherub* 1974, *Stato D'Animo* and *To Claudia* 1990, and *O Father* in 1991.

Part One takes the reader to the poet's familiar Fitzroy Park and Carlton Gardens in Melbourne; or we walk with the poet through the dark and damp forest with the *mighty mamaku* and *wet fronds* of New Zealand. In another the poet asks the question, *Where is Hugh?* suggesting majestic eloquence through man in action – a poetic encomium to my son, Hugh, a solo mountaineer taken by cancer in the prime of his life. In another poem *Upon Prejudice* he reflects on a world of aggrandising prejudice, *the crystal artifice / the meretricious vein*, and a search for truth in *Board and Lodging*.

In lighter vein he returns to a little sparrow chirping on the back of a chair with the use of vernacular language in the last few lines; and *Now and Then* where a poet minimises his very existence as a writer. *Old Songs*, with its passing parade by a river-bridge, and more particularly the three poems, *The Sparrow, His Love will Show a Way* and *A Day in the Life of* find a vignette form. In *Two Poets* he dialogues with a host of poets from the past; in another there is an old man walking in the rain juxtaposed with thoughts of artist David Hockney, with his blue swimming pools of California; and in *Casa Sorolla*, a little jug bubbling in a room takes the reader to a long-dead Spanish painter whose pools and sounds of a *thousand violins* evoke this poet's garden in Auckland – *nothing more onerous than that*.

In September 2012, well-known New Zealand artist, Don Binney died: *A Lifetime* is a fitting and sensitive tribute to that artist's sensibilities. *Ohakune New Year* was the first poem written in 2012, and the last in 2012 was *A Day in the Life of* which found form in Swanston Street on 29 November, the hottest November day in Melbourne for over a hundred years; then in February 2013, on the road between Auckland and Ohinewai, during a long hot New Zealand summer, two more poems came to life: *A Short Fall of Anarchy* and *Whatever we Strike Out*.

In Part Two we are in the world of the child: *Poems for Wonderment.* There the reader can delight in the imagination of the child and these poems are best read aloud. *Peach and Cherub* and *Daddy* were written to his own small children in the mid-1970s when he was a young parent; more recently, *For the Child* was scribbled on the back of a napkin in a Melbourne café. Others follow. The poem *To Charlotte* grew from conversations with a friend's daughter Charlotte; *Funny Things* permits the child's pure and unfettered imagination; *Thump Thump* deals with a child's fears by exposing and incorporating them in a fresh and safe way; and *A Short Fall of Anarchy* takes us right into the moment of childhood daring and trepidation.

Nick writes with unwavering reverence for language, be it legal language or the intimate journeys of the human heart. Ultimately the score belongs to the world of language where every note brings on the whole sound as the poet scans and limits to create. Overall each poem testifies to *the running of words / the handshake language makes / and even enjoys,* and when, as readers, we close the last page we might wish there was more to run with.

In *A Life In Poetry* Professor Michael Peters spoke of "the artful constructions of a writer to make everything beautiful in its simplicity" and another critic in the *Melbourne City News* said of his poetry, "it is agreeably accessible and sparsely beautiful, evident of an excellent eye for detail."

We can only hope that this writer continues through the *last lap* to call on this excellent eye, and to open the world of his observations, his intersections, to make us stop, look and listen to ourselves and others in another way. No inveigling angst, bare of cynicism, only the art of an uncensored, accessible uncertainty.

Part One

The Returning

The Returning

So I stood listening
and before me a voice.

We all shall return one day
run the stillness back.

Where the thirst calls
there we will wander with no weariness
    before night falls
    stalk
    with no one
    by no one forbidden.

By summer trees
    and no one
    tumble
By winter leaves
    gather
Linger by a threaded bearded fountain
and a long grey stone building
    elbowing the fountain's mist.

By a golden elm
smell streams and clinging leaves
    share the shedding thoughts of night.

From sombre-shadowed wall
    watch the fabled thrush
    singing swallowing dipping
    or stand motionless
    the tawny owl camouflaged to perfection screeching
    the wild drake meandering on dark water.

From cosy corners of compliance
    walk the time with me
    find those faded bluebells in the wood
    a picture
    from soundless childhood hours.

[Cont.]

And in the returning we shall hear
the old bridge rattle
a duck's beak scrape
the water to the weed
an earthworm ease
a pathway to a home.

Hockney Bright in the Morning

An old man with light in his eyes, white in his hair
Without lie, with a tie, with a sigh
Lays his umbrella on the floor.

It's raining outside the watertight wigwams
And gaudy gallery walls –
After a while of words
With a dislike here and there
He shuffles off with his umbrella
Hunched a bit against the shops and cold.

The skies above the glistening road are uninviting
And his old hands are cracked and wobble –
He was adamant the girls drank too much and he used
A good word about them that I forget.

There he is heading towards Mt Hobson
And he found he had begun to like and then
Really fell for Francis Bacon –
We talked about that.

And from my watertight corner
I saw a pale painting of *Mr and Mrs Clark and Percy*
How Hockney wanted white Blanche there with white lilies
That's how the light gets in
Reworking Claude Lorrain –
Though I couldn't think of David Hockney's name unrehearsed
Or describe astutely his clan or mien
Till I just thought he saw light ahead of angst
Cooked an innocent arrangement and found
The swimming pool blue of California to make much of.

From a blue swimming pool and by a local wet road
With light in his eyes and white in his hair
Someone holds his purpose
No glamorous moment
Like a poem of an old man.

Two Poets

Today over the horizon a woman carries chickens on her head
Elsewhere in windowless rooms some practise capricious nobility.

The door is open
the bee is busy in the now still flowers
all the muffled fretting moments
are drawing to a close
all blends in fitful ecstasy
the black night falls on silvered tracks
sliding on a McCahon waterfall.

Is this the time?

Left alone when I was in the sand hills
was I running from reason?
Falling where the sea-sand sweeps and sings
sliding lupin to lupin
sand trickling over walls and paths to a grey road.

The winds turning by shop bins and litter
scurrying by grave steps and flowers
waiting for a pure morning
words waiting
the jewel of children left eloquent.

Something in me is running from prejudice.

Left alone by the long afternoon
clouds burning bridges across the sky
where the stone clock still harries the seconds
and closes the hours
I head home.

Will poetry bring me back?

He eats lunch slowly at a white table
the doctor-poet I meet in Hawthorn
we have forgotten our small space

at most we amend the embers of our past
leave Rilke, Pessoa, Nietzsche
as we swallow sauce and peppered spuds and cream
and split the white crumbed fish
and the white plate bare.

Inside chance we safely sit
without moving from our corner
hearing the chasing muffled thud of the word
our meeting our cover.

Listening to one another
Modigliani drinks copiously to Laforgue and Baudelaire
good-enough Whitman moves aside for Pushkin
every word agreeable to the time
and time again.

In another room pale travellers
track to find chairs and comfort and skirt the endless hum
the dimming means and corner light
to leave the luggage of a scoffing world.

Somewhere a woman carries chickens on her head
In windowless rooms some sedulously practise capricious nobility.

Maillol turns his fingers to the stone
Mallarmé rings the bell of night and death
lost Lorca turns to gypsy truth
the naked shingles of the world
seek Matthew Arnold out
Sandburg passes by.

In Parnell a world away
a Chinese cello player tells Coral
how beautiful her flowers are
snagged convulsions in the wind
coralled by a white picket fence and pavement.

The shadow of a moment seals
And I have met the poet fair, there and there, and here and here.

To Dylan Thomas

Greenly I saw him grow
    As though in lucent spot
A symphony in sadness cropped,
    Entered all the time
His soft-rose ears and eyes
    His soul sunrising in the skies.
I thought to make my bones to his notes,
    With green-heart mind my hands spoke,
A poet-bud bare effloresced
    Preened by those of greenfulness.

Greenly I saw him grow
    As though in lucent spot
A symphony in gladness cropped,
    Entered all the time
His soft-rose ears and eyes
    His soul sunsetting in the skies.
He thought the palest stirrings in the mist
    As virgins' yearning amethyst.
He did not reach nor mock nor sing
    The right to mountains bared to sight.

For Claudia

I miss my Swiss miss of the Mount
forever I remember the stranger with round eyes
and the long legs with her German poems
and how first she read one out
about a handkerchief with a tree by a lake in it,
which I corrected her was not *in* but *on*,
and the poet's last line was that
no one could laugh if he could not blow
his nose on it
and he had a very German name
which kicked off every verse and from
memory there were four.

And afterwards I ran down the Mount
with no shadows behind me
and pushed the key into the ignition
and drove home to write about
the Swiss miss I did not miss
on the Mount that beautiful day.

Where Is Hugh?

The mountains give us clues:
incompletely revealed
some men, pale, chastened, frowning, slink along.

You reached where the world
never could catch up with you
the cerebral, the physical, the lover's man
ahead of all such abstractions
you climbed above grey harbours of obscurity.

You saw Einstein connections
before our commonplace registering
with acuity and rhyme
this was your time.

Climbing shining summered in snow and snoozing peaks
some you abandoned clueless
ice shelf long and sharp
as the naked reason of your mind.

In thrall you calculate the tearing of the avalanche
the cry of the crevasse
warnings burnt by the passage of wind-torn ice
the oxygen of your lungs and longing
turning to the mountain peaks
beyond our beyond.

Step by step
glimpse by glimpse
to the flesh of the mountain side
you played the risk and rhythm
it levelled you
emboldened your heart and spirit
held your purpose clear.

In the footsteps of the nurturing voice you climbed
shouting to a piercing untold power

I chance again
I risk again
I dance again.

As soaring peaks called
above the scorched and cluttered world
you left whatever wrangling.

To the world of a steep overhanging
you took your chances.
On corrugated plains below a mother stirred
her song singing for you.

But not alone across those peaks
in that wild free somewhere else
you hold brothers living brothers loving
tumbling the lanes of childhood
unmonitored laughing spilling down a grassy bank
all atoms longing for a day's last scream
morning chills and evening thrills
to take to flight again.

Now, this now, where are you Hugh?

Beyond the reader and the writer
you return this day
a heart in hiding no more
and through the hurt of tears
silent as a star
take her aside
tell again a sister of sorrow
that beyond the stars
you found a better climb.

Often cruel but true – the turning:
the inside cell takes man before his time
a hurt in hiding no more.

Upon Prejudice

The reader wakes to the awakening word.
    What avers? The dinkum word?
    Let us be modified
    let the words take up the pursuit
    position the train of words.

Poetry a rare intuition
    owes nothing to technical cast or fortune
    but carries a cache of words possessing a life of their own
    alien accidental lucid lawless
    lightning-bright strikes
    on the frontiers of complex gesture
    loosely hovering.

With tender corrections
    defer the vanity in the everywhere
    however badly burns this irksome trial.

No need to levitate
    beneath the staircase old worn racquets and reels lie
    drop the heavy suitcase
    close the cupboard door
    the ducks in flight forever tall
    revolving on the family wall.

Be grief-full of the mind
    together remove abstruse offerings of no little obscuration
    thwarting the running of thoughts
    halting the running of words
    the handshake language makes
    and even enjoys.

A recklessness is here
    entailing the loss or gain of our being.

Time to bypass this hesitation
    curtail this clamorous commodity
    for platters we offer to prejudice
    for this palaver we protect here and there
    as gods descending from heaven hoping.

In sunlight bypass humiliation
    sweep the old stones clean
    sail the placements out
    fix ourselves a cup of tea
    hear the deep grottos sigh.

Pigeons are cooing in the grey-toned square
    time to throw away the crystal artifice
    the meretricious vein
    the sinking dreams of spring
    and by sweet nothing rue the stain of pity.

What need to steal the boneless crest or crime?
    From Pompeii and everywhere
    constrained or unconstrained
    stones are cracking
    cracking the craven artefacts and tombs
    where cold cart tracks have long held secrets.

Board and Lodging

I hollow myself out: for speech is strange.
O vision of the loneliest, Zarathustra cries.

Even if it's the father don't trust fully
O may the voice of truth be heard again
    even a whisper
      against the chatter of evil tongues
      and the clatter of bombardment.

But if you love truth attune your ears
    for just like lies
    truth lives because of those who listen.

No truth without ears
No poetry without truth
    no vision of surrender
    all vision of the circumstance.

Aren't we all here because we want to hear it
    and find /retrieve from a furious flood of falsity
    the frail flotsam of truth?
    A lot of F's here Hélène.

Shall we succeed? I don't know
    but I hope and think so
    I think the whole thing is quite exhausting.

My presence here now before you
    is an act of faith
    long delays expected.

Forgive me acts I have committed
    I beg like a beggar who sells fresh books
    the whole act is quite illuminating Hélène.

Does the truth lie concealed somewhere?
    Will it lie in wait
    or will it simply lie?

Short-sighted as most humans are
    we don't always manage to find it ...
    a slow spider in the moonlight
    weaving through the stars.

This spectacle of hers and mine I dedicate to truth.

We will begin to gather
    when we know our sheltering
    and maybe truth will find us
    holding onto bewilderment.

A deed knocks first at thought
    and then – it knocks at will –
    that is the manufacturing spot
    says Emily Dickinson.

Author's Note
In this poem-conversation I am indebted to the many
thoughts and words of French writer Hélène Cixous.

Stato D'Animo

To be left alone
by a long rolling beach
when you have left me
with a boat shed and a jetty below me
and the grasses blowing in the wind.

Like a single blade of grass
surrounded by air and spirit
if I surrender my importance.

Shall I surrender to this time
alone without you
or am I already closer to you
when you know me
as the grasses, the sun, the far islands,
waiting in this space of little reefs,
waiting in our time, outside the soft unions,

irridescent in an anchored ark
to surrender, to die down,
to be alone
by a long rolling beach
letting my brain bump quietly
as the stranger's boat in the bay
with a boat shed and a jetty below me
and the grasses wheeling in the wind.

Where does a gold-drawn moment come from?
How does one hold the bronze thoughts?
Where to place the dam?

I will not leave the place
where the sea waves take off for other spaces
where sails that slip the long-fingered headlands by
bring a bride of peace and silence
on a tide of polished light.

Where the sun slides on the tide's back
today I feel the rain on my face

and the bride of peace
has spread her heart to me.

Mind Fever

I must go down to the pub again
    To the bar and a cooling beer
And there I'll let the minutes fly
    And toss the weight of care.

I could go back to the church again
    To see where the eagle stands
And I will hear those organ notes
    As though from a distant land.

I may go down to the sea again
    To the call of the waves and the hill
Where I could live in worthy light
    And need not pray or swill.

I will run down to the rocky shore
    At the urge of a surging tide
And there I'll find a poet's place
    Where life and words reside.

I must go down to the sea again
    To the moving sands on the shore
Where I can snare a seabird's song
    And will not ask for more.

Author's Note
John Masefield's poem 'Sea Fever' captures my attachments to
the sea and the old breakwater at Sumner. My childhood was
spent fishing here, below the hill at Scarborough, and being
part of the roar of the tide.

The Launch

On the occasion of the launch of A Life In Poetry
26 September 2011

If maths means not a lot to me
    nor aromatic funny tea
What I like is when the words
    hassle me to point absurd.

So when tonight you've vanished, gone
    and whether held in love or scorn,
I'll say to Lizbeth on our porch
    "Not another bloody launch!"

And she will say with wryest smile
    "Hang about, and write awhile –
Who knows what litter in your way
    turns to gold another day!"

For should you like a ditty witty
    show the poet pious pity.

Break a smile and you will know
Shakespeare always ran the show
    and homeward happy you will go!

Ohakune New Year 2012

I swallow
    from the red books
    re-read all the virgin words
    lawful missals of sons past
    drink all shames
    try the horseradish at midnight
    welcome the needless time.

Here I am a stranger to be seduced in my own tracks
    beholden to the mighty mamaku
    sovereign rimu and matai
    scarce of sensitivity
    I tread among
    the perching epiphytes and snaring supplejacks
    waiting they hold me back
    mysterious.

Footsteps disturb the slumbering fronds
    muddied
    green no longer
    the moss on forest floor.

From below the vine-lifted skies
    I hear the winds
    my ears sprinkled with leafy dew.

Old travellers from consoling paths
    sow your own heart
    seek freshness
    the wish sticks.

Coming from nowhere
    going somewhere
    we don't know where
    booming
    a train shredding the drifting mist.

From the corner *Powderkeg*
    all dreams spilling
    those smells of revelry
    hallowed in roadside hours.

In the middle of midnight
    a rocket blasts
    cows retreating
    a moon misshapen glabrous
    slips along the rooftops
    glancing on A-frame edges to settle on our road.

By the mountain over-bridge
    lucky in his moment
    a weta waiting in dark corners
    a water rat advancing from his labyrinth
    a hedgehog thrown too hard to see another day.

Hear from the asphalt
    it is six o'clock in the morning.

The waters from summit Tahurangi
    flow quietly to the sea.

Winds are turning where the world has gone to sleep.

Author's Note
Over many years I have been privileged to be able to pick up and read a history of Dr Elizabeth Grierson's A-frame chalet at Ohakune by Mt Ruapehu. These writings and holiday adventures over thirty years are recorded in four or five volumes with predominantly red covers. And I have read the mountain exploits and memoirs of many families who have enjoyed the ski base and mountain walks from the chalet. Poignant are the written records by both Hugh and Campbell Grierson. These memories I make reference to in the first verse of the poem.

From Casa Sorolla

To Joaquin Sorolla, artist, 1863–1923 Valencia

On a wooden floor in the room
the little jug is bubbling busy
steam pressing the paint-splattered easel.

And through the doorway
Sorolla is looking at the water
and with southern eyes
perhaps he is seeking the movement of light.

In the rain on the pavement
tap-tap goes the blind girl's stick
but you and Sorolla
can see reflections in the pool of his earthenware pots
and verdant leaves.

You can't see the blind girl's mood
she is listening.

Life is a reflexive art
shifting and still
still and shifting.

Engulfed in flowers and shadowed silences
leaves running on leaves
on the rim of the world
I open the front door to my garden
all spreading below the grey drapery of the sky.

I swallow the moment
my eye pushes past half-shrunken flower heads on the path
slides to a gap in the trees
where gregarious fences and gutterings merge.

Beneath the pots and three waterfalls
Sorolla sees prowling bows upon the water

goading the strings of a thousand violins
that's what Sorolla is seeing today
silvering the flowing water.

From my front door
I hold a teacup stained by invention
(know she is tapping somewhere)
as the paint slips and stains and all swims together.

Everyone is pushing their luck
their broom their friction their reflection
poets are pushing their words
the pages are pushing back
sable brushes squiggle their signature
paint wrinkles and dries on the canvas.

By the doorway leaves are falling
wrapping the edges.

Drawn to a dawn
an old man is looking for his glasses in the morning
nothing more onerous than that.

The Starter's Gun

It's hard to congratulate the world but I will
and the sun and the moon and the stars
I will leave out of it
leave the lowly sheep to graze and the dogs to bark
banish the silvering enchantment
bright buoyant shards of light after rain
sweeping the mists of meandering rivers.

So what shall I look at awash with passion in a glass?
The way my bones creak in the morning?
I don't think so
nothing memorable there
that allows me and you to go somewhere else.

They look to love
they talk of it
they talk endlessly it seems.

They hear the sounds of many tongues and coalesce.
They look to wealth but where?

At the pull of the tides
host the day we are steering to
this the hour we are staring at
whatever the stars or pain.

So together let's make a start
spit the pith and dreams
tread the mud of the ignoble track
congratulate today
find in our exact moment
the residue and retinue of ruin
the hope beyond the hope
the thought that holds towards today.

Gathering sheltering
resurrect that thing called love
and see what happens.

No message no wonder
with eyes of chilly silver
the starter's gun has sounded.

All or None

All poets are mad
they hang about
when there is nothing to hang about for.

All poets are sad
they hang their words out
like washing to stiffen and bleach in the wings of the sun.

All poets are bad
they leave their washing on the line too long
until someone bumps their head on the sheets
and curses the words for being there
interrupting their lives.

But poets are wearing the words in their heads
their heart on their sleeves
their sheets in the wind.

Should they do this?
Couldn't they quietly die in the demands of dirty washing?

His Love will Show a Way

Though last week's rain has freshened
      fresh flowers
I was nuts about her spicy smells
and how religiously her feet turned in
and her head bowed when her smile lit up
      and her mouth slumped as she laughed

put another way
her simple black dress
runs to a palatial hotel
relentless mesmerising chaotic

      in Room 204
      my fogged brain put to sleep
      and she disappeared after that

the economic elasticised maid
her pauseless knock
like a hovering helicopter or scratching wasp
was accompanied by

      you could have folded the brocade back

I could have

      or I could have picked flowers in the rain

O Father

What do sane men expect from the sea
when the ship is sinking?
Fine if you find not fury:
even a dead sea drowns.

O father in a drowning sea
you have let me feed off your time
and warmth with wine.
Now whose words shall I fire off?

You had the chance to punch the wall
or did you want to be divine?

Where I have Witnessed

I have it at last ...
thank you for the things
you have given me.

Thank you for the fields and fellow travellers
        and for letting me finish my journey
        this way to just here.

I can't leave it there ...

Because some have found me
        fashioned me
        fathomed me
        they know the gift they have been.

Don't cross them out in your perfect plan
we have all found each other out.

I did not expect you to love me
        more than I loved your world ...
        there I have witnessed wonder.

My last lap is longer than I thought
        far or near the foe
        far or near the end
        don't tell me.

The cursor you have moved
the gaps in my life
        you have filled with wonder.
        thank you for having me.

Old Songs

Monica says malapropisms are excusable
when people feel a need to try too hard.

After the shriek of the city
outside mixers and means
windows and bars in acrid stain
mean words mustered to snare
the proud chintz chased by the sun
Descartes' ramparts holding badly ...

you think of things down by the river
the weight of the city in your wake
the way things pass or stick
like wet shoes from last week's rain.

How seriously
the man on the bridge
book in hand for who knows what pursuit
sets up shop
sheds a soliloquy retaining lonesomeness
Christ in every detail spinning the planet
and by implication a loving Father
ferrying our offences.

But the little girl with braces
is getting used to her glasses
today's focus routine tears
maybe her culture will cross-reference
I don't expect so.

See the proliferating helmets making deals
with who knows what God
the strollers strolling
the rowers sweeping the waters
fast-food papers floating
old hearts walking past conflict
young breasts beating

the old beggar buggered by torment
wowsers left laughing
as the long day slips by and night presses.

Today bridges are bridges
air is air
and the bridge is above me
the river steps take me down
the river steps take me up.

And maybe that's what the plan is all about
old songs left beneath the arches.

The Sparrow

Love doesn't wait for the sun to go down
listening for love we let go.

So I am watching the little sparrow
chirping on the back of a chair
as I suck on my iced-coffee straw and listen
and wonder what antennae he had cranked up.

And by a brown river
the doors of the food-hall
opened and shut
shut and opened
and often for no reason – you know what I mean.

But the sun shone and the girls strode
they seem to know what they're about
and the seagulls just seagulled
swooping and squawking
and some shadows slid and concrete set.

So I scraped the chocolate out – and the cream
and with the last sip he came back and chirped again.

Then a big broad white shirt squatted and
squashed the place he had perched on
that's how it goes.

I will write it down with smoke and cigarettes and discarded dreams
and like so
by dint of
it goes like
well – like with smoke and cigarettes.

A Lifetime

I thought him a genius at King's.
Sometimes words speak another word
        whatever we think or speak.

Sometimes they suggest.

The bird flies or stands
cries for plain words – like life and environment …

It behoves poetic wisdom to let them
        give off steam, allow wingbeat
        allow the wind
The words and wages to wake and stream
Strewn on canvas fast in glorious line.

        You can hear them, see them
        catch them
        nothing seen?

And sometimes, not always, the spilt words
        are best not mopped up
They fall and lie in wasteland
        they lie in wait
They are waiting to be given ascension
To join the procession in the Binney birth canal.

Sometimes paint and words rhyme in time.

Author's Note
Don Binney OBE was one of New Zealand's most admired artists and conservationists. He was celebrated for his consummate images of New Zealand birds and the coastal contours of Te Henga, Bethells Beach on Auckland's Waitakere Coast. He used language well. His death on 15 September 2012 aged 72 was sadly noted by many New Zealanders. His prodigious talent I first met as a schoolboy at King's College in Auckland.

A Day in the Life of

footpaths extra hot now
like my *Golden Tower* flat-white
and my silver metal watchstrap
    makes my wrist itch
    I like it off

there on the table
time ticks without me
    and all those camera images still wait and shimmer
    by the Princes Bridge

and my wig of sweat
attests to the boiling railings
    it's 3.30 pm
    and a Melbourne station is insisting
    somewhere it's 39 degrees

at fast trot a tram is heading
back the way I've come from

but a black and white dress with long legs
and deep voice
is leading him over the tram tracks
    she's cutting across
    to the verandah coffee place opposite
    and fierce to her plan
    is gathering him up
    saving herself from his sullen wisdom

I can't help wondering
if sudden decisions were necessary
on a day of heat and crawling inexactitude
    when she had murmured 'don't you want to?'

I lever myself
gather up my glasses and newspaper
push the metal chair in
to the coffee-maker nod

collapsed in the weight of his own heat-wave
    remember my watch
    and the time
    the black and white dress

Author's Note
To Ursula who inspired this poem on her return from Denmark
and London with her new black and white dress. Her direct
engagement with life did the rest.

Whatever we Strike Out

To write about the Age or run the Moment
To clear the air and greet calls to emptiness
To dare to dance in clouds and storms
To simply empty-start and try free-wheeling
Leaving the siren-calling
The has-been fingered way.

To catch the garrulous winds in branches
To be free to settle for less-not-more
To be less feeling-self less breathing-self
And free the slave-in-wanting
Locked inside.

Once more to know our cells can be as dry
As the water-tank on the rising hill
The nursing ochre swept and rushed by fire.

To realise our time was all time
To know we need the rain-power
Our shapeless air-power to take-off.

To swirl to move aside
To settle for the love-power
Again to know the path-of-love random unpatterned
Does not always pass through love
To know and welcome falling-wonder
Rolling rescues-in-love …
The petty curses we excuse
To out-enchant
The wave-ice-frozen eyes.

Bread-life-take is wonder
The crumb too is wonder
Whatever we take death will dance.

For an Earth taken by a rose
Do the rains seek approval
Or the sun for his next-day stalking
The moon for her remnant mien and mystery?

Death comes too early and too late
Rolling down the ochre-hill
Time's not torn
We were born for it
For the love-bites and the frost-bites
And the light that dazzle-slights and bites.

To know and welcome wonder
Without anticipation
Without the avalanche
Without mire
To know wonder whatever we strike out.

The finitude is now and waiting
Reverberating to fruition.

Author's Note
This poem was completed on 27 February 2013, 99 years after
my father Terence was born. I thank him for the gift of words.

Part Two

Poems for Wonderment

Pa and Nick on Wooden Horse
Maurice James Gresson and
Nicholas Lyon Gresson
19 December 1943

A Short Fall of Anarchy

When I tipped the water on you Grandpa
it was a poem I was writing
from the second floor sash window
it was the way the water sped and splashed upon your head
those were my lines my plans.

And, I nearly forgot,
it was the way the light caught the water falling in the air
before it met its shiny target.

I'd phoned you earlier to come and see me
a real note of urgency in my voice
and here you were along the road, through the gate, across the grass
approaching the nursery door, the two steps.

And I hiding upstairs in the spare bedroom
couldn't resist
lining up my target …

But Grandpa, it was, I think my heart that spilt
and it was my legs that ran and rushed me to a dark place
not to the shade of the old pepper tree.

And when we met downstairs in the playroom
you never mentioned my poem
never exposed the waterfall
the drowning anguish above me under me
the fresh mind that froze.

For I who fluttered in a firefly's beam
was seen, was seen.

For the Child

I'm going home today
Said the bedpost to the rice
So could you let the hedgehog in
And give him back his dice.

I'm going bad today
Said the lettuce to the doctor
So could you turn the talking off
And ring a helicopter.

I've got to ring today
Said the tiger for a plumber
I'm in a spot today
I expect the proper answer.

I've got to shop today
Said the teapot to the chimney
And when I've had a smoke
I'll finish all this whimsy.

I've got to stop today
Said the washing to the driver
And anything you think I've said
Well, telephone the tiger.

Peach and Cherub

A Peach and Cherub came to stay
They stayed and stayed and stayed all day,
To pinch poor Daddy's nose in play
A Peach and Cherub came to stay.

A Peach and Cherub went away
They thought they'd take a holiday,
Daddy had a boring day
When Peach and Cherub went away.

A Peach and Cherub reappeared,
Daddy has a brand new beard,
To pull that beard was quite absurd
A Peach and Cherub plainly heard!

A Peach and Cherub stayed away,
They caught a glimpse of life's array,
Beloved, how soon the time for play
Is years and years and years away!

Funny Things

One day I saw a pussy cat
 Pounce upon a mouse
When Daddy made him let it go
 It ran around the house.

It crashed around the kitchen
 It skidded on the floor
Can you guess what happened next?
 It scampered out the door.

One day a wrinkly elephant
 Hid behind a horse
He thought I couldn't see him
 But he was wrong of course.

One day a yellow tall giraffe
 Was jammed inside our shed
When Daddy went to get a spade
 He got a fright instead.

Next day a hippopotamus
 Dived into our pool
And when I went to have a swim
 He said, "That's not the rule!"

Today a jumping kangaroo
 With Joey in her pouch
Hopped in through the kitchen door
 And sat upon our couch.

When Mummy brought the shopping in
 And put it on the bench
She saw the naughty kangaroo
 And started speaking French!

One day a busy buzzy bee
   Buzzed into my room
Poor Granny broke the window
   When she hit it with the broom.

So when you go to bed tonight
   And thoughts run through your head
Remember all the funny things
   And giggle in your bed.

I nearly forgot
   That's not the lot
      My darling sweet forget-me-not.

And when you go to sleep at last
   With pictures in your mind
Of kangaroos and funny things
   Such happy dreams you'll find.

And then you might remember
   When you snuggle in your bed
How someone pulled the sheets up
   And kissed your little head.

Daddy

Don't think of Daddy never here
    But free to come and go,
You only have to close your eyes
    For you to make it so.

Just curl up in your bed tonight
    And pull the sheet up tight,
And soon you'll hear old Daddy plod
    Down the hall tonight.

Think of Daddy loving you
    And all the things you said
That brought the sparkle to his eyes
    And made his face quite red.

With just your arms about your head
    You'll feel him always close,
For Daddy is the one we see
    When there is no remorse.

Nobody Knows

Nobody knows what the old witch knows
Nobody knows where the old witch goes
    into the forest, into the trees
    perhaps to feed the birds and bees.

Somebody said they saw her once
Somebody thought, perhaps a hunch
    someone not exactly right
    heard her prowling in the night.

Somebody saw, somebody knows
Someone spoke her heart of woes
    someone in the seamless dark
    heard the hurting in her heart.

Somebody feels, nobody knows
Exactly where the old witch goes
    but someone not exactly mild
    knows the secret of the Child.

Author's Note
*By the stream that flowed through Gartmore, Mrs
Mulcock's house huddled alongside a dell of mysteriously
tangled vines and strangely growing tree-trunks. I was
the child who saw her, a bent figure in a black dress,
carrying an axe to cut kindling. Nobody ever spoke to
her. The back windows of her little house were covered
with cardboard. Later I found out she was not a witch,
just a lonely widow – and I was sorry for that – but
that is what the child sees.*

To Charlotte

Charlotte was a little girl
    and quite devoid of guile
But sometimes things can go amiss
    so listen just a while.

When Charlotte said that 10 x 10
    was equal just to 4
Miss Toogood made an awful face
    and screamed, "It's much much more!!"

Poor Charlotte went to school next day
    and was assigned a sonnet
And when she faltered, stumbled home
    a bee was in her bonnet.

When Charlotte went to school next day
    she had a dreadful fright:
Her teacher turned to her and said,
    "I understand your plight."

"When I was young and went to school
    I wasn't good in class
But I have learned to persevere
    and get it right at last."

So little ones who feel concerned
    can heed the golden rule:
There is no need to be afraid
    just love your time at school!

Thump Thump

There's a ghost in our house
    And he goes **thump thump** banging around on the stairs
And I shiver in bed when I hear **thump thump**
    For I haven't a clue why he's there.

I haven't a clue why he likes our house
    Do you think he has relatives here?
Do you think all the time he is looking for friends?
    But I haven't a clue why he's here.

There's a ghost in our house who goes **thump thump**
    And maybe I'll meet him tonight
But Mummy says nobody goes **thump thump** ...
    And I wonder if Mummy is right?

Next day I was playing at chasing
    When I tripped at the top of the stairs
Then I slid all the way to the bottom ...
    Can you guess who was waiting right there?

He saw me, he smiled, and he chuckled
    As I bounced all the way down the stairs,
Can you guess who saw me and caught me?
    It was **Thump Thump** my friend who was there!

So now when you hear all the noises
    You will know there is nothing to fear,
Just remember if ever you're falling
    Thump Thump will always be near.

I'm a Poet

I'm a poet at an airport
I'm a poet in the bath
I'm a poet when I'm dripping
I'm a poet when I laugh.

I'm a poet when I'm thinking
I'm a catcher of the words
I often race to find them
They're all I can afford.

I'm a poet when I struggle
I'm a poet when it's apt
But words are never easy
To find or to adapt.

Can all of you remember
When you catch a favourite verse
While reading through the pages
The poet got there first.

Postscript
Elizabeth Grierson

Reflecting on this volume, I suggest that in Nicholas Gresson's use of words, as per the evaluation by Sir Arthur Quiller-Couch in *The Oxford Book of English Prose*, there lies an indebtedness to the English language, with its *speech malleable and pliant as Attic, dignified as Latin, masculine, yet free of Teutonic guttural, capable of being precise as French, dulcet as Italian, sonorous as Spanish, and of captaining all these excellencies to its service.* (Cited in 'The Magic of Words' by the Rt. Hon. Lord Justice Birkett, from his Presidential Address to The English Association, UK, July 1953).

Then I turned to American poet, Robert Frost and read *The Road Not Taken*, and the last two lines spoke to me of Gresson's life and poetry:

I took the one less traveled by,
And that has made all the difference.